About the author

Meiling Jin was born in Guyana in 1956 of Chinese parents. She came to England in 1964. She visited China in 1981 and was deeply moved by the experience. Her interests are wide and varied. She is a black belt in karate, enjoys T'ai Chi, and has worked in very different jobs. She has written several children's stories and is at present working on a children's novel. Some of her writing has previously appeared in the *Funky Black Women's Journal*. This is her first published collection, and it promises not to be her last.

o my lover who
are introduce me
to poetry as well
a turning my life
around
yours with a lot of
affection. '78
CW.

Gifts from my grandmother

poems by

Meiling Jin

illustrations by

Hiang Kee

First published by Sheba Feminist Publishers
10A Bradbury Street, London N16 8JN

British Library Cataloguing in Publication Data

Jin, Meiling
Gifts from my grandmother.
1. Title
821'.914 PR6060.I/

ISBN 0 907179 44 4

Typeset in Plantin 10/11 by Lithoprint on 249 7560

Printed and bound by
Cox and Wyman Ltd

Contents

Introduction

I wanted to ask someone famous to write the introduction to this book of poems so that it would be a bona fide poetry book with a glowing introduction. However, as I didn't know anyone famous, I chose to write the introduction myself as I know better than anyone else what I want to say. The poems are about my experiences, as I see them, and as I wish to record them:

Further thinking then led me to the truth:
'there's nothing like taking responsibility for what you have to say.'
And another truth:

'you have to fight to speak. Otherwise, a sociologist-anthropologist-historian, or even an ideologist (and usually a white one at that) will think they have the right to speak for you. (the nerve!)'

For me, writing is healing. It is also communicating. But above all, it's powerful. When I think of the mass media and the mausoleum of dead white poets, who have such a hold on people, I feel diminished. It's as if, I am hurling myself against an enormous concrete wall; the only dent being to my head.

However, one of the reasons that keeps me writing is the thought that someone might read it and be able to find something in it to connect with. I can never forget the first time I picked up a collection of stories by women writers in China today. It was the next best thing to talking with them. Writing is powerful. It gets across ideas. And there is always the chance that you might reach someone.

About this book of poems, the theme, if there is one, is self-discovery. By self-discovery, I mean the making of a connection with something that is essentially yours. This is not a once and for all act as the self is always changing. It involves process: discovering, discarding, owning. By making these connections we can touch our own power and from here, begin to make changes.

So here is what I have to say. I hope you will find something to respond to.

I came to England from Guyana when I was 8. My parents chose England instead of Barbados[1] because my uncle was already here and it seemed as if this was where the new life was. My father came first and we followed later. The year was 1964, and we were leaving a very unstable political situation.[2]

The night before we left Guyana, we went to Georgetown and slept like refugees on a bare wooden floor. I slept hardly at all through fear, and a gold bracelet that dug into my hand. The bracelet was a memory given to us by our grandmother, one each.

I did not enjoy the journey by plane. It was long and bumpy. I remember the stewardess telling us to swallow something called, 'your saliva'. I did not know what this was but as I was chewing the gum my mother had given us, I swallowed that instead.

1. *They thought of Barbados because the weather was similar. It was nearer too and perhaps when the situation in Guyana had calmed down, they would return . . .*
2. *Read any book by Walter Rodney on Guyanese History or "Racism and early childhood", in The Funky Black Women Journal. Issue 1, May 1985, published by the Black Women's Writing Group.*

When we arrived at Gatwick Airport, England, it was the beginning of June and the weather was freezing. It was all very strange. I think I must have left speech behind because I did not speak for days.

Our family, seven of us, lived in a room near Earls Court. We went to the park during the day and came home in the evening. Sometimes, we ate lunch at our aunt's flat and had sandwiches when we got home. I enjoyed playing in the children's park although I was wary of the other children. They seemed nervous of us.

My father used to go out for days looking for a secure place for us to stay. He must have been worried because winter was coming and still we lived in the same room. Eventually, he found somewhere — a maisonette above a shop. And so we moved, the seven of us, together with two of my aunts, their husbands and another uncle. I think we must have slept head to foot. A real squash but I didn't mind. I liked the warm comfort of so many bodies together.

When I first went to school, I was shocked; partly at the indiscipline and then at the backwardness. I was writing proper writing while they were still printing. But, in order not to be different, I took to printing.

I did not enjoy school. I hated the other children because they never ceased telling me what a freak I was. My sister and I were the only Chinese people in the school. We fought a lot with the other children: mainly the boys, who followed us home from school. They used to form a circle around us and we had to push our way through. When my sister left that school, I took to walking home the long way round.

The most important teacher to me at the time was Mr H. He taught arithmetic and he was an Asian man. I had no friends for a long time and, inspite of the crowd at home, I led a solitary and unsupervised life.

When I was about 10, I discovered the Children's Library. It saved me. It was a complete fantasy world and it was quiet. I liked quiet. I started reading round the Children's Library from left to right. I discovered Dr. Doolittle, Crimson Fairy Tales, Indian Fairy Tales. And then ballet books. One after the other I devoured them. Fortunately for me, I missed Enid Blyton. Her books were kept in a special place to the far right in front of the librarian's counter. By the time I made it to the counter, I was already making a strange and sudden leap to Coleridge, Bernard Shaw and Wordsworth. I learnt chunks of the *Ancient Mariner* by heart. I liked poetry from very young. I liked sounds that rhymed and I liked words.

Today I enjoy writing poetry. It is versatile and economical and a form of expression that comes easier to me than most others. This hasn't always been the case. I got here through a round about route and largely by accident. I have found the English language to be a straight jacket. The imagery is white (grisley grey, black hole, snow white and pure, in the blackest hour ....) The form is white too (14 lines make a sonnet ...) only the feeling is mine. There is a certain Wordsworth way of expression (*I wandered lonely as a cloud* ...) that seeps into my writing and determines how I express myself. But what can you expect. I have had a diet of Dr. Doolittle, Shakespeare and Georgette Heyer. From this, I would throw out, or rather spew out things. Until I changed my diet to women's books: Fay Weldon, Marge Piercy, Chocolate Waters. Then I found myself in a straight jacket. Couldn't get it out. Then I changed to Chinua Achebe, Naipaul. Nothing happened. Then I discovered Maya Angelou. And then the Woman Warrior, Toni Morrison, Audre Lorde, Kitty Tsui and Alice Walker. And then I began to write. I write because I want to. Because I have to. And even after this, there lurks the white ghost of Wordsworth somewhere. (These things take time). But I have called a truce now with the Gwei lo[1] and with the English language. They must stay in the mausoleum of obscure objects. And we must continue to write and to fight to get our work published.

... with love and thanks to the Black Women's Writing Group ... Zhana, Ingrid, Dinah ... and the Chinese Lesbian Group ... and Ilona ...

1. *white ghost*

A woman appeared to me in my dreams.
She told me
to stop talking
to death
and get on with it.

The Journey

And then i died.
They placed my body
in a boat
and put it on the River.
There, it travelled rapidly
down stream
and, being taken by the current,
it drifted deep into underground caves.

Rowena,
can you see the sunset?
Mama,
can you see the sunset?
Sister Sally,
can you see the sunset?

i no longer see
the sunset.
i am travelling
in a boat
along underground caverns
journeying..

strangers in a hostile landscape

Strangers in a hostile landscape

When people ask me where I come from
I tell them this story.

I was born in the Southern Hemisphere
in the early hours of the morning
when night exchanges with day
and the light gains ascendancy.
What I have to say is brief,
so listen,
and make of it what you will.

When my grandmother was a girl,
paddle-boats crossed the river
from the town.
They brought all sorts of people
looking for
God only knows what.
Unspeakable riches, I suppose.
Instead, they found sugar-cane;
sugar-cane and mosquitoes.
They worked hard on large plots of land
dem call plantation.
Slaves worked the plantations originally
and when slavery was abolished,
freed slaves worked the plantations.
And when they were decimated,
we worked the plantations.
We were called,
indentured labourers.

My grand-father sailed on the ship
Red-riding Hood:
part of a straggly band
of yellow humanity.
They severed the string
that tied them to the dragon,
and we grew up never knowing
we belonged
to a quarter of the world's people.

A damn plot you might think.
Yes indeed, it was called,
colonial-ization,
spelt with a z.
The prince of the plot was called Brit Ain
but actually, he had many brothers,
Holl And, France and so on.
They fought each other occasionally,
but essentially, they were intent
on making themselves rich
thro' robbery and by brain-washing us.
They stole from us.
And at the same time,
sung psalms.
Such sweet sweet psalms
and sung so well
wash the sweat and tears away.

After much time
and many millions of £s later,
they leased us back our land
through a deed called In-Dee-pendence.
This meant the land was ours,
but every thing we produced,
was theirs.
We even got our own leaders:
men of great worth
to them.

Meanwhile,
another plot called Imperial-Ization
had worked its way through the world
and the earth was carved up
and re-aligned.

Back on the Plantation,
we all fought each other
(with a little help from out side).
We squabbled over what would remain
when the In-Dee-pendence deed was passed
and the prince departed for home.

And so,
in the midst of the troubles,
my parents packed their bags.
They followed the general recruitment drive
to the imperial palace itself.

We arrived in the Northern Hemisphere
when Summer was set in its way
running from the flames that lit the sky
over the Plantation.
We were a straggly bunch of immigrants
in a lily white landscape.
We made our home among strangers,
knowing no one but ourselves.

When I was a girl
I lived in a box
that is why, my head is square.
I lived on jam
and played on the streets
I survived in this hostile landscape.

And when one day
I was chased from school
I turned and punched their teeth out.
Too harsh, you say,
I don't agree,
they would have smashed
my head in.

One day I learnt
a secret art,
Invisible-Ness, it was called.
I think it worked
as even now, you look
but never see me.

I was born in the Southern Hemisphere
in the early hours of the dawn
and when I die
I shall return
to a place I call my own.
Only my eyes will remain
to watch and to haunt,
and to turn your dreams
to chaos.

Those were the days

Sitting in the sunshine
eating advocado pear sandwiches
watching my mother play
with her favourite grandchild.
It hasn't always been like this.

There were the days
when there was no food.
when she served over the counter
fourteen hours;
when we moved from one place
to the next.

I was afraid in those days
of never being able
to meet the morning,
being stuck in the twilight
of the day before.

Never knowing
what catastrophe lurked
around the corner,
I lived in fear
of the landlord.

And a dimly lit room
with paraffin heater smells,
a woman sobbing, sobbing.
Your brother's broken the sink
O God, what shall I do?

Those were the days
when 3Ks were chalked on our wall
in large red letters.
Go home
Yellow dogs.

I'm going home, sir
yes,
right now I'm going,
going in my mind,
going home.

Those were the days
of fearfully clutching at straws
of eager hands grabbing
the last piece of fruit.
And as I watch you
I fear
this is only the intermission.

On anger

Anger.
Where is my anger?
Hidden under the chair
In a box
On the shelf
Deep within
It lies hidden.

Release.
Touch the hidden knot of anger
It seeps out

Lash out
Lash into the night
Smash it in.

Rats

I hate rats.
They remind me of teeth-marks on the bread.
We used to cut round the teeth-marks
And eat the bread.

Baked beans and rice

Dear mother,
did you ever realize
how cham chong*
baked beans and rice was?
I'm sure we children
didn't either.

**mixed up; cooking term for two things fried up together.*

Soya sauce

....

You'll never change, my girl.
You still eat soya sauce
with every thing.

Chinese Take-away

I will take away
a chinese,
lock him up
in a pentonville
for serving food with lice in.

That will cure
his presumptiousness
and maybe even
his gambling.

Fried lice,
spare ribs,
crazy yellow bastard.
Why can't you be civilized
Just like us (er) british.

(And anyway,
I have to get rid of my hate somehow.)

The Knock

Where shall I lay my head?
House and home have I none,
Nor country yet to call my own.
Once I thought my home was here,
But now I'm told that
By some Act,
I have no right to live
in peace.

I have been
right round the globe.
Not a traveller by choice,
But one who has been dispossessed.

I live in fear of the knock
That knows no mercy.
Swift and suddenly it comes,
And I, behind the door,
Wait trembling.

And quietly comes the Dawn.
The knock.
Police.
A short trip
Via the airport.
A oneway ticket
To an unknown place
Called Homelands.

struggling

One of Many

i used to be a Chinese Social Worker
but now i'm just a Chinese,
one of the many
living here in Britain.
We go about our business
on the fringes
trying to make ourselves thin enough
to slide past your malice.
Or thick enough
to absorb your hatred.
Or transparent enough
to go unnoticed.
Some of us are deeply wounded,
our bodies litter the landscape.
We did not make it past your malice.
Our eyes betrayed us,
and the spikes stuck.

I get around

Do i remind you of
someone else
who was a nurse?

a nice girl

Did you see me
on TV, you know
what's that programme called?

Have you met
my sister Kay?
She's just like me
she's studying to be

a nurse.

i'm sure
you might have seen me
somewhere:
serving you,
or nursing you,
or cleaning up
your rubbish.

Yes madam,
we *do* look alike
and we even eat dogs
where i come from.

My mother's hands

I don't wish to
Eulogize
My mother's hands.
But
I must admit
They are,
What you might call,
Beautiful.

Thick
Rough
Calloused
They may be
From holding so much pain.
I don't wish to
Eulogize.
But they are
All the same,
Beautiful.

Shopping

I can't define that feeling
of your eyes
on my back
stabbing into me.

Did I steal from your stall?
Did I hit your little daughter?
Did I kick your dog?

Do you dislike my nose?
(which you hardly ever see
because you never look at me).

Or could it be, that you despise

my Blackness.

No more fighting

I can't fight with you sister, anymore.
I will talk with you
And share the pain
But I won't fight with you.

We argue
And shout
We beat each other on the breast
All the time.
And we're so busy
We don't notice
Gwei lo*
Come and take
our children away.

I will not fight with you sister, anymore
For the road's too long and hard
And I need all my strength
To stay on it.

* *white ghost*

Rowena vs the tribunal

RAGE
I,
am full of rage
for what you did to me.
You,
make the rules to suit your selves
then sit in judgement on us.

What is it you're saying?
'We are not guilty
of attacking your integrity,
taking away your identity.
Perhaps it's your hysteria,
incompetence,
idiocy.'

I listen in a daze
full of rage and distress
at your ignorance, arrogance
and placid violence.

'Stand up Rowena.
Stand up and listen to our judgement.
After much deliberation,
We,
who sit in judgement,
do, most solemnly declare ourselves,
innocent.'

Fools
I think.
You who lie
and wrap yourself in your deceit.
You who perjure your own soul
with your lies and complacency.

I look into your face
and see nothing.
Not a single thing.
An empty, desolate landscape.

You condemn yourself.

Divide and Sub-divide

Dear Miss
Ellaneous
Please state
Whether you are:
Black- Asian
Black- Afro
Black- Caribbean
Black- Chinese
Black- Of mixed origin
Black- Middle-Eastern
or Black- other.
(Do you mean to say
there's more of you?).
If Black- Other,
Please state which.
This is important
For us to know
Although
It is
Highly confidential.
We shall not
Disclose it
Even to
Ourselves.
We simply wanted to
Know
So that we might further,
Divide and Oppress you.
Sorry
Cancel that last remark.

Old Black Woman

Old black woman
sitting under a tree
in Euston Road.
No home.
Only a few bags.
She munches on
a pack of crisps
and watches
the young
white offices workers
school children
business men
and others
walk past.
She chews slowly
each crisp
and inhales
the car fumes.
She listens to the noise
and watches
a solitary leaf
float down
and crash to the floor.
See it all.
Seen it all.
Life is vicious
to poor
old
black
women.
Especially here,
in white England.

disaster

When the nuclear disaster comes
I don't know whether
I might have the strength
to run for cover.

For by this time
I shall be dying
of bad housing
bad diet
complete lassitude
and madness
too weak even
to hide my head under the blanket.

But when my body explodes
into millions of fragments
I'll be gone you people.
Just my dust will remain
to choke you.

Bankrupt

Have you ever wondered why
My voice is edged with fear
When i talk of the children
And the dreams they will inherit?

Does it make you want to fight?
Or lie and howl in the night?
Or push it to the furthest edge
Of your brain?

Give them organic carrots
Tell them not to breathe the lead
And still they will inherit
A sunless world.

Your mother is lying.
She has no answers, only stones.
We were bankrupt quite some time ago
You know.

Yet another poem of struggle

The poems that tell of struggle
are all written.
And yet i find us writing more.

More struggle
More poems
And no end in sight.

Only the desperate

Only the desperate
need apply for assistance.

For the desperate
are desperate.

They clutch at your sleeves
and your trouser leg.

They hang around your neck.
They follow you incessantly.

And try to steal
into your dreams.

There is nothing beyond desperation
only despair

And beyond despair?
Motivation.

To Anna

Poor Central America
Struggling for its very life.
We could write many poems
And obituaries
To each one that died
Except
There is not enough paper,
Or ink,
Or tears
To fill the sprawling gap
Left by your deaths
And lives
Destroyed
By a single bullet
From the North.

We can only mourn
Send arms
And wish
For their destruction.

The Boat Girl

When I heard about your pain
I wished you dead little girl.

Running from the war, a casualty.
Fleeing the bombardment in a boat.

If only you had died then
My little sister.

Instead of living
To tell the tale.

Seven times it was. Seven times raped.
And thrown into the China Sea.

Yellow rain

Yellow rain is a flower.
Her stem droops and blossoms yellow.
She calls to mind our soul
And brings joy.

Yellow rain is a poison
In Vietnam it killed many people.
It reminds us of our soul
And its destruction.

Dead monkey

A dry shrivelled up monkey
skin barely covers bones
starved to death
(disgusting).
Sun will dry it out further
and then the carcass
will be light enough for wind
to scatter it.
Back to the barren earth carcass monkey.
But no,
not carcass monkey even.
A closer look reveals,
a child,
a dead shrivelled up child.
Carcass child,
or carcass monkey,
who will care?

Hope

Pheonix soaring in the sky
Burning a path across your heart.
And, from the ash emerges:
A charred bird.
Poor Pheonix.
Hope has to be fought for it seems.

No more new dawns

Gone is the magic of the early morning
Instead is a mist that hangs on my chest.
Acid rain disturbs my brain
Lead and smoke chills my soul.
Enthusiasm is dead;
Killed by the axe
Of your complacency.
Tell me, is your silence catching?

I look around and all I see is
Desolation.
Desolation and oppression
in my own Back yard.

And over the fence?
Namibia.
O Namibia,
What have we done
To you?

Lady bird
Lady bird
Fly away home,
Your children are starving
And are,
The victims
of mass genocide.

From my stupor, I hear the shout,
Wake up!
The eleventh hour is past
And we are fast approaching
The End
Of the day.

And there will not even be,
A new dawn.

love poems

Mani in the asylum

I dream your face
No longer contorted by fear.
Instead,
It gazes peacefully out
At those Eastern Hills.

Yesterday, long ago,
You sat,
Huddled in the corner
The grimness of this place
Eating away at your soul.

More than mad you were
Beside yourself
More like
When they took your will
And crushed it.

You were never one
To tolerate
Their viciousness.
You fought back
The only way you knew.

And when their walls
Could
No longer contain you
You took yourself away
Back to the Hills.

Spirit gone now
Body buried deep
You lie
Watching and waiting
For the Hills to move.

A poem to my dad

It hurts me that sudden severing:
You disappearing into timelessness
Without me even knowing it.
It hurts me something terrible.
Is it the disappearing?
Or the not knowing?
Because you never Said Goodbye
I still have certain things to say
Many things left unsaid
(Our lives are said things anyway).
And for all the pain we shared
I would have liked to say that time.
Goodbye
God bless
And thank you.

Friendship

Here's to friendship
Long-standing,
Unremitting,
Quietly waiting,
Worked at,
Left,
Fought over.

I would build me
A black box,
(In the wood-work class)
In which to preserve it.
Except that,
It's not containable.

My lover's sheets

My lover's sheets are green,
a soft soothing colour
and when she holds me,
i feel safe enough to sleep.

Black Tulip

Yesterday i saw a black tulip.
It reminded me of your mouth
and how much i enjoy
kissing.

Your lips

Purple
        indigo
purple
        indigo
indigo
        purple
purple
        indigo.
Indigo
        indigo
indigo.
Dark
indigo.

Your lips
are full.
And dark indigo.

One for the storehouse

The fading evening light;
Your face
deeply engrossed
in a book;
The stillness
and the noise
of the sea;
All this,
will I put
in my storehouse
of good memories.
And hold it
against the coming storms.

Passion

....

Passion I will not let you
Rule my life.
For fear that when you
Leave.
I will remain an empty shell
Of reproachfulness
And anguish.
Far better turn my face from you
And walk along
Cool Monastic Courtyards
Boring.
But pleasant all the same.

Lovers

Cry, for the death of something in us
Let's say innocence,
When we loved without knowledge
Of each other.
When to each other
We unveiled
The hidden parts of ourselves,
We both stood back
In horror and disbelief.

Gathering Distance

It started slowly,
imperceptibly,
this distance.
One layer
and then another
until
you disappeared
altogether.

Parting

We didn't get there
You and I

Look long and deep
Part ways

I don't know how
We came to this

Except I feel
A vast nothingness
Of grief.

Gone

My lover and i have goodbye
and the pain i feel
is greater than
a shaft of light filtering through
drawn curtains.
It falls on the empty place
where she lay.

Unbroken silence fills the room
and nothing i can say or do
can fill the gap
she leaves behind.

Lay down memory.
Go to sleep.
For, you cause an endless flow
of water from my eyes,
a lurching feeling deep inside.

Lay down memory.
Easy now.
That i might bury you deep. Deep.
And sleep away the pain.

Loneliness

Loneliness is a friend
who, when i go to bed,
lies next to me.
And as i drift between waking,
and sleeping,
she hovers on the edges
of the night, in silence.
Watching. Waiting.
And when i wake,
she greets me.

Secret Woman

Are you the woman
i dreamt one night:
came to my house,
spoke with me,
into whose eyes i gazed,
and between us passed,
something,
i'm not sure what?

Or was it someone else i dreamt?
Or am i dreaming now,
of a strange, secret woman?

Like ships in the night:
a temporary respite
from this loneliness.
On the fringes of
i and i

A question of mistake
i did not feel your hand
softly stroking my back,
or your eyes,
gazing into mine.

i only dreamt your tenderness
as i lay asleep one night
waking
dreaming
wishing.

connecting

A long over-due poem to my eyes

Poor brown slit eyes
You cause me so much pain
But for you, I would be,
Totally invisible.

When young,
You filled with tears
At the slightest provocation.
When children teased,
It was because of you
They hated me.

In story books,
Her big blue eyes opened wide.
But you, you narrowed into slits.

Hard brown slit eyes
Echos of the pain
You mirror back the world,
And I can see them all,
Drowning there.

Soft brown slit eyes
Windows of the Soul
I can see you staring back
Frank, open, lovely.

Soul loss

Brinking on the edge of pain
teetering on the abyss
you call
i draw back.

When i was a child
a demon came
and stole my soul
all he left was an empty shell

i wandered around
lost
looking for the demon
looking for my soul

i fought emptiness
despair
anguish
i took to aping the demon.

Until, i found a naked flame.
i walked through the flame
and met the demon
grinning at me

He held my soul
between finger and thumb
and dared me to
step closer.

i hesitated.
He grinned
i crept closer
he opened his jaw

i crept closer still
he held my soul
over his open jaw.

i sprang on him
he swallowed my soul.

i teetered on the brink
of despair,
and ate him.

Fear

Fear,
i no longer
have
the strength
to hang on
to
you ..

You
have
moved
within
my orbit
making
a total eclipse
of my strength.

But,
being
tired
now,
i
let go,
And
feel you
slowly,
disappearing

into
space ..

My Sister

The last time I saw her
She was trying to catch
The Sun.
Her right hand clung to
The rail of the boat
Her left hand clawing at the sky.

What is it,
Said I,
That you're trying to do?

I'm trying,
She said,
To hold the Sun
For a moment
In my hand.
For then,
I shall be
Neither happy
Nor unhappy;
I will cease
To be.

It's impossible,
Said I.

Yes I know,
Said she,
But I must try
All the same.

I never saw
Her again.

Poem to Ailin

To you
vulnerable
yet so strong.
When you set your face
to the East
I can see
Many women standing there.

Ruth

Ruth, a good Jewish name.
Your namesake,
a good woman of Moab.
Loyal. And no doubt Black.
Even though,
whitewashed over the centuries
to a delicate shade of brown;
a suntan no doubt,
got from working in the fields
gleaning barley.
But we know better Ruth,
King David was Black.
And you, a strong woman,
stand visible.

Louise

When i first saw Louise
She wore old dungarees
car grease on her hands
smudges on her face.

When i first saw her
that night,
i said to myself,
my sister.

Whether we like it or not
we are,
Yellow Sisters: dykes by birth
and much more besides.

i won't parcel you up
into a neat box, Yellow Sister,
but many things
link you to me.

Memories of swimming the Essequibo
for a bar of chocolate.
walking on the sea wall
looking for crabs, we connect.

Or is it your eyes?
your slanted eyes,
your dungarees,
your 10% discount for Lesbians.

A hostile environment
links you to me Louise:
it strikes a cord
in our own deeper selves
when our eyes meet,
in recognition.

Matilda

The day Aunt Matilda died
Fog descended
And coated
The wet Autumn streets
As if, in apology
For her existence.
She left nothing behind
Only a cat
And a plant
Which she cared for religiously.

She was a poor spinster:
A lesbian some say.
Her life had no meaning
Except,
For an out light burning slowly,
In the dying evening light.

Still more hostile

The old ones are dying,
Making way
For another generation
Of immigrants.

This landscape
Sapped their strength
and remains,
Still more hostile.

Grandmother Ho

My granny was a chinawoman
With big feet;
They never bound her feet
Because she was a peasant
And had to help on the land.

I remember her, hardly at all
Except for the bottles
Of strong dark liquid:
Cure for all ills
From toothache to uppityness.

I see her sometimes in Chinatown.
Here and there,
An old, yellowing woman
Walking slowly,
Because of her arthritis.

I wish I had paid attention then
To her memories
(for she had plenty of memories);
Instead of filling my head with books.
And she never was in any book.

My granny was a fine woman
With strong hands
And a good sense of humour.
I see her in my mother sometimes,
I see her now in me.